AC Benus

Demon Dream
poem

*"We live in succession, in division,
in particles. Meantime, within
man is the soul of the whole; the
wise silence; the universal beauty
to which every part and particle is
equally related; the eternal One."*
— Ralph Waldo Emerson
(from the essay "The Over-Soul")

an AC Benus Impression
San Francisco

Grateful acknowledgement is here offered
for the support and encouragement
I've received on the literary site
www.gayauthors.org.

ISBN 978-1-953389-13-8 (ebook)
ISBN 978-1-953389-14-5 (paperback)

DEMON DREAM:
A POEM.

Cover photo:
Joseph V M / pixabay.com

Vignette:
Caveman / wallpapercave.com

鬼の夢

叙事詩

Demon Dream
prelude

Once, when an old woman came to perish
   As truant exile on a barren plain,
Her fragile limbs snapped, not letting her rise;
   So in the spiteful dirt she writhed in pain.

All the fear she still composed, feared this death.
   Being cut off now, she fought that unknown;
Though it drained strength and stole the time still left,
   She fought for it, for what else had she known?

Remembered, past memories began to rage,
   The woe of life, a moment to endure:
From father who sold her, she ne'er forgave;
   To the man who took, ne'er thinking to love her.

Only a life of toil unrewarded
   By child or hope stung her dying thought,
And all the dreams condemned yet unfilled
   That the younger heart of hers had once sought.

Her husband, dead some twenty years ago,
  In a fever's fire, sailed on like a sigh.
Smiling in happy wonder, he passed on,
  While she now contended hard not to die.

An unseen thing stirred and drifted in the air,
  Drawn from the Heaven Shelf down to her strife.
Her fear of death delivered her a hell
  In semblance of a deal for mortal life.

Old and alone, a woman came to die.
  In a heartless room, the night of her brain,
Crept wonder of what life had signified
  But drudgery and love betrayed through pain.

In a dream from which she should not arise,
  Her savior whispered, and a compact swore.
Fretting, she took it that life should not end;
  She feared death, but woke more doomed than before.

Demon Dream
poem

I need a new master;
A new and better one!'
The servant's mood was tried
And worn out through travel.
Now this desolate road   5
– Just a ribbon of dirt –
Seemed to be the last straw.
'Didn't he consider
The late hour we struck out?
Now, stuck in the nowhere;   10
No people, no houses,
No place to bed, no...oh.'
A new thought hit him hard.
'Nothing for my stomach!'
He glanced up at the man   15
Walking in front him,

The re-hashed notion come:
'I need a new master.'
The plains surrounding them
Were broad and summer-parched,   20
With a hazy network
Of peasant paths and trails
Crisscrossing the base of
Mount Adatara's slopes.
By the route they trod now,   25
Ajisai grew in clumps,
Their wide leaves insect-chewed;
Their stalks crowned by hundreds
Of flowering blue sprays.
But servant, Tarogo,   30
Couldn't bother to care.
'All we have to eat are
Hydrangea for dinner!'
His foot kicked a large one,
Sending azure showers   35
Of pollen in the air.
A malevolent turn
Made him strike a neighbor.
His glare again beset
His master's back ahead;   40
The servant's eyes narrowed
To but disdainful slips.
'If he knew my thinking,
I'd never live to see
Employ under a new   45
Master and family.'
But servant, Tarogo,
Was very much in error,
For out in front, master,

Yukei, was absent of 50
The taint of bitterness.
For, quite the opposite,
Yukei's thoughts had been swamped
By all the sights and sounds
His hired man had ignored. 55
He thought of ajisai
And their earthly brothers,
The plants and blooming buds
Reaching ever upwards
For a light never touched. 60
How they stretched, even though
It burned them in this drought.
Yukei *looked* where he trod
And felt refreshed by his
Perennial outlook 65
Of young optimism.
Here in this light he'd felt
The air 'round him enrich:
Turn from tinnish yellow
To deepen copper-gold, 70
So that now he could watch
The sky finally set
The fields afire in orange.
'How like the human soul,'
Yukei's wide-eyed wonder 75
Considered the matter,
'These little moments are.
One microcosm is
Another soul's cosmos;
Each separate, running smooth 80
In a much larger one,
Yet in blind harmony

With the spec'lative whole.
It is light within dark;
Chaos amongst order;   85
While still every being
Retains the memory
Of the much smaller place
From which it chanced to spring.
It's how we remember   90
The womb as paradise;
And up and up it goes,
Until we may at last
Recall God's entirety
Is in all that sprang from Him....'   95
"Master," Tarogo said.
"It is getting dark, sir,
Shall I light the lantern?"
The master, peeved at this
Interruption of thought   100
By the interruption
Of human speech, replied,
"Save the candle to use
Against the coming night,
Not the still-glowing dusk."   105
His wisdom, needlessly
Pointed to chastising,
Had itself been rebuked.
And in the instant out,
Yukei perceived the flaw   110
As but a gnawing trait
He would daily battle
To rid from his nature.
"Tarogo," his tone sang,
"What goes on in your head?   115

Won't one night on the ground
– With all the sky of stars
Admitted as bedmates –
Be a damn sight better
Than your usual spot   120
On an unseeing and
Sterile, unmoving floor?"
He then added quickly,
"And can't you imagine
A night without your meal   125
Will provide your system
Some much needed cleansing?"
The master's face then smiled
While his finger reached out
To poke Tarogo's ribs.   130
His servant stared at him
With a lost-for-words look.
"Yes, sir. It's true," he said,
But in his head, he thought,
'I need a new master.'   135

~ * ~ * ~ * ~ * ~ * ~ * ~ * ~

Some one hour later,
The trail growing dimmer
With each footfall they made,
And the shadows taking
The last hue from the plants,   140
Tarogo stopped to light
The wick in the lantern.
It was while he was stooped
The sound first came to him.
Nearly toppling over,   145

Thinking the meadow grass
Had somehow conjured song,
And was singing to him.
He jolted to his feet,
But Yukei raised his hand   *150*
To keep his servant hushed.
For deep from within the
Sea of switchgrass prairie,
The men could hear a chant
Rise as faint as if from   *155*
The crescent moon inching
Above the waves of green.
"Listen," Yukei then said,
"We'll let these strains of song
Be our guide and loadstone.   *160*
If the people are good
To wayward travelers,
They'll offer us shelter."
Room and board, Tarogo
Had no objections, but –   *165*
What irked him was Yukei's
"If." If they were good folks –
But then, what if they're not?
Lantern-less they started;
Stepped off the relative   *170*
Safety of the roadway
And into the dark wilds.
By the time the moon had
Traced a part of the sky,
The travelers' progress   *175*
Made them appear as two
Dismembered heads floating
Atop the rustling grass,

Ever following on
To where the singing led.   18
Entering a clearing,   0
They stumbled on a shack
Which, from its roof of thatch,
Seemed more straw than structure.
From the house, a clearing
Held the wild plain at bay   18
In all directions by   5
A dozen yards or so.
Otherwise the grass would
Consume the thatch of the
Little house carved from it.
In the quartered moonlight   19
Casting blue character   0
Of the haziest sort,
Contrasts of height and width;
Of ground and growth, diffused
A rounded appearance
To every opposite.   19
And all moaned in pleasure   5
When the night caressed them.
The singing was louder
And more mysterious
As its notes blended with
The natural world which   20
Couched it in such beauty.   0
Tarogo, uneasy
As the first to see this,
Got a shock when he turned
To Yukei behind him;
He'd sort of forgotten   20
Anyone else was there.   5

Instantly recovered
Once more, his eyes grew round
With fearful panic that
He had been rude to his   215
Own earthy provider.
He humbly begged pardon.
Coming 'round to the front,
Yukei then boldly stepped
Into the clearing and   220
Cupped hands around his mouth.
Towards the shack's front door
He shouted out calmly:
"Greetings unto this house.
May we meet the one who   225
Dwells within this abode?"
Within, the enchanted
Siren voice drawing them
Barely wavered a hitch
As it sang its eerie   230
Tale of ancestral woe.
However, when the door
Slid on its frame a bit,
Letting flickering spill
On the colorless ground,   235
The song faded away.
In the modest doorway
Stood a frail old woman.
The two traveling men
Looked on with mouths agape   240
For the peasant appeared
Quite old indeed as she
Got down on creaky knees,
Assuming the perfect

Attitude of deep-bowed 24
Humility to them. 5
"Dear grandma," Yukei said,
Stepping from the clearing
Into the door's squared light.
"Such formality's not
Warranted on a night 25
As lonely as this one." 0
Helping her stand, he asked,
"Gran, where is thy husband?"
Now to Yukei's glancing,
The deep-furrowed wrinkles
Of the old one's face showed 25
Heroic endurance. 5
"Oh, master," she began,
"Please forgive me, but he
Died a lifetime ago."
Assisted to her feet,
The slightly winded lord 26
Bid Tarogo step close, 0
For he'd stayed by the grass.
"Dear, gray-headed lady,"
The master assured her,
"You have nothing to fear
From I or my servant." 26
'Or,' Tarogo wondered 5
Silently to himself,
'Had we better her fear...?'
But within an instant,
The thought was driven off.
Yukei started once more. 27
"We've travelers who've lost 0
The day and guiding warmth,

For thieving petty night
Would steal our fuel, but give
No direction in turn.   28
May we rest our worn bones   0
By the hearth that comforts
The ground you inhabit?"
She glanced slowly, shyly
From one man's hopeful face
To a second less sure.   28
To Yukei she replied,   5
"My lord, those of heaven
May find it a sore task
To wrest some rest from earth,
But what little I have
Is at your disposal."   29
Her timid utterance   0
Then stooped with her into
A truly humbled bow.

~ * ~ * ~ * ~ * ~ * ~ * ~ * ~

                                                    29
Warmer now, the travelers   5
Stretched 'round the *robata,*
Or the sunken hearth
Of the main living space.
Half the shack was mud floor,
Compacted down rock-hard,
Where messy things were done –
Including the cooking.
Where Yukei and servant   30
Reclined with outstretched legs   0
Was where the old lady,
Or indeed everyone

Known as 'down to earth' folks,
Spun and smoked; dreamed and died.
Tarogo's mind drifted,   31
Seemingly with the smoke,   0
Up to the charred rafters
Being licked upon by
Feeble light from the fire.
When the old woman spoke,
Both men felt the surprise.   31
However, her tone stayed   5
Meek as a mouse and asked,
"May I spin? In this way
I earn my livelihood,
Master, transforming flax
To the yarn my neighbor   32
Exchanges for the rice   0
And vegetables I eat."
Lifting her silver head,
She watched the firelight
Play upon the features
Of the men so different.   32
Tarogo's type she'd seen –   5
An average man was he
Of earth, wind and water –
The kind who'd complain of
Heat in summer, and cold
In every other month.   33
His ambitions were tied   0
To the endless cycles
Of his gut and stomach.
But of Yukei, she knew
His mind was more starry;
And more set on finding   33
                                                      5

What some might call a soul.
"Don't let us bother you,"
Yukei said graciously.
After she bowed and rose
To bring close her distaff   *345*
And bundle of fiber,
Tarogo whispered nigh
In his employer's ear,
"Master, I think this crone
Is hiding food from you,   *350*
So that—"
            "If she has food,
I will surely not be
Partaking of any..."
Yukei paused, realizing   *355*
The other's true intent.
He scolded: "Nor will you.
I'll see to that myself."
The threat was delivered
To keep his hired man   *360*
On the straight and narrow.
Kowtowed, Tarogo bent
His head muttering with
Apologies; all while
His stomach growled insult.   *365*
The old one drew up to
The *robata* once more.
She set about her task,
Spinning a bobbin raised
With her one hand, around   *370*
Which trailed loose strands of flax
To be gently drawn by
Her other hand into

Twisted linen thread fine.
This completed product   *375*
She'd occasionally
Turn on a wooden spool.
Mesmerized by her work,
The men sat silently,
Helpless to look away.   *380*
Knowing this, the woman
Softly began to sing
An ancient fairytale,
Sending her voice up like
Smoke amongst the rafters,   *385*
Where it'd eventually
Drift across the fields.

 "The old man set his trap
  And in it an old badger caught,
 Whose feet all a flip-flap,   *390*
  The man to his old woman brought.

  Badger, Badger,
  Tied up tight for the soup,
  Unloose the knot
  And you'll know what to do.   *395*

 'Here!' He held up his prize.
  'He ate our food, now we'll eat him,
 For every creature dies
  Despite brain bright or dim.'

 'I'll place him on the rack   *400*
  For you to make tonight's dinner
 When I come tumbling back
  To feast richer than a sinner!'

Badger, Badger,
See, she's easy to dupe;   405
You know the spot
To work and slip on through.

With that, the old man left
    And the woman went back to pound
Wheat with a pestle-cleft.   410
    'Untie! I'll help you grind it sound.'

'Think I'm a fool, do you?'
    The woman asked. 'To the field you'll
        run.'
'That!' said he, 'I'll not do.
    You've caught me fair and square, and
        won.'   415

Tired old fool was she,
    She set the Badger to her aid,
But by letting him free,
    It was an awful price she paid.

            Pestle, Pestle,   420
            Cracked her skull in one swoop –
            Badger, Badger,
            Go and heat up the pot
            And with her stew
            The starved old man, his soup." 425

While Tarogo reclined,
Re-hearing this old tale
He had known as a boy,
He thought this opening

Of the story gruesome 430
And perhaps a local
Variance on the theme.
All he knew was of how
The clever young rabbit,
For love of the old man, 435
Got Badger's punishment.
Rabbit's revenge he knew.
The two visitors felt
At ease and comfortable,
While under them, the wood 440
Flooring around the hearth
Brought heat from the embers
All through their bodies.
For, although it was June,
Mount Adatara's heights 445
Sent down the craggy slopes
Untimely chilly air
From the higher heavens
To the meadows and plains
Encircling its base. 450
Yukei relaxed, but watched
The widow at her work.
The process intrigued him,
For she'd follow the same
Procession of movements 455
Time after time again.
Each action was unique,
An individual,
And discrete from those that
Came before and after; 460
Each inducing the grace
Of dexterous virtue

Inborn to it alone.
He wondered why people
Couldn't behave the same,   465
Selecting the right move
To apply at the right
Time without the malice,
Often arbitrary,
And applied with just force   470
Enough to reach its goal.
"You do that beautifully,"
He heard himself tell her.
A glance at Tarogo
By the old lady proved   475
That man's eyes were napping.
Puzzled, she asked the lord,
"Sir? What is it you mean?"
"It's your spinning I mean;
It's done with deliberate   480
Grace in every movement."
He added, "I feel it."
Her reply was humble:
"But it's just what I do.
I don't think about it."   485
Yukei nearly sang back,
"Yet that is the reason
Your spinning has become
Artless and beautiful;
Become part of your ways,   490
As natural for you
As the way you breathe, or
Find a stride when you walk."
He paused, wondering if
She could follow his thought.   495

"You," he went on, "have found
A kind of peace in what
Your hands can make for you."
She scoffed silently then,
'All my hands have made are   *500*
Calluses for my hands.'
She rubbed her right thumb o'er
The hard yellow skin corn
Grown dead in her right palm.
These were something she thought   *505*
The man in front of her
Would never know about.
"There's no joy in this, sir."
She dared to raise her eyes.
"I'm too old to feel love,   *510*
Or likewise to feel hate,
For the things I must do."
She half-expected her
Irreverent words would
Stir ire in the man.   *515*
But he merely remained
As calm as he had been
For the entire time.
Conscious now of staring,
She returned to her work.   *520*
Once her rhythm was back,
Yukei said, "Life is more
Than fueling our bellies.
What good is existence
If it finds no place home?   *525*
For every animal
And, yea, for every leaf
Has a part within it;

That perfect place where it
Finds that it belongs, and   *530*
Nothing in life's rhythm,
Or in life's dying can
Forget from whence it came"—
His gaze sank to the floor
—"Except mankind, who feels   *535*
His definitive loss
As inexplicable
Longing, which churns over,
And over until it
Is able to assume   *540*
A shape – much like your yarn –
That he only thinks has
Value for his efforts.
And if lucky, if rich,
He pays other people   *545*
To do the job of life,
And they, like your flax, get
Spun into one long line
Of lumpy, soulless men.
They who fear death, I say,   *550*
Are the ones who've never
Lived for any others.
For, to the ones to whom
Death means the reunion
Of themselves – along with   *555*
All-receiving Nature –
They know death a kindness
To accept when it comes."
He glanced up to her with
Enthusiastic eyes.   *560*
She replied demurely,

"But, forgive me, sir, if
I comment too sharply,
But I've never had time
To enjoy much of life."   565
"Well, then," he said, "forgive
My rude tongue and bluntness:
That means you've never lived."
His bright eyes would not leave
Her face, and he hoped she   570
Had seen what he had meant.
For in his mind he knew
It was never too late
To start enlightened life.
But, the old woman's thoughts   575
Choked on her bitterness.
Who was he? A noble,
Reared on a coddled life
Of staid, urbane studies
To tell her – a woman   580
Born to toil and to sweat –
That she didn't know what
It meant to be alive.
'If only,' she then thought,
'We two could trade places,   585
He'd know what life's about.'
As deferentially
As her rancor would let,
She said, "I work to eat."
He responded slowly,   590
Realizing too late
How his jovial tone
Might have antagonized,
Although not meaning to.

More contritely, he said,   595
"I know our allotment
Upon this world has been
A very different one.
Mine born to be 'master,'
Though not a distinction   600
I sought or exploited.
From you I claim no want,
Except for some knowledge.
For once I was like you,
In at least one regard,   605
And lonely as you now.
I grew up with no friends,
And my books taught me how
To expel my own fear
When it was not called for;   610
But what I sought in them,
And what I could not find,
Was the essence of me.
I could not find myself.
How did I fit into   615
The universe 'round me? –
What purpose did all the
Chaos around me serve?
The moment I found it,
I forgot the question.   620
Forgot I'd once not known."
His smile was back in place,
This time, a kinder one.
"Know, my good woman, that
The moon revolves for you.   625
The sun rises and falls
For you in the same way.

And every blade of grass
Grows in your eyes alone.
Because, as you perceive   630
everything in this world,
So it has been and is.
Be happy, and all that
You encounter will be
Every bit as happy.   635
Tranquility finds rest
In knowing this supreme.
Believe this is as sure
As your forthcoming death."
Yukei glowed in the light,   640
And more than the light could,
For his whole presence moved
With a thousand movements,
Each one shot and quickly
Counterbalanced by force   645
From an opposing one.
All gathered in the strength,
Lit by the firelight,
Of a man at perfect
Ease with himself, and All.   650
Tarogo lay asleep.
The old one saw and heard,
But had nothing to say;
Words could no longer speak
A single thing for her.   655
What she most desired
Was for her guests' comfort.
With that as an excuse,
She clambered to her feet,
Saying, "Masters, please sleep.   660

And when the morning comes,
I will make us breakfast.
Only"—she cautioned well,
Regarding the awake
Tarogo on the mat—   *665*
"Promise me while I'm gone,
You'll not open that door."
The men looked where pointed.
Yukei held her frank eyes,
Then nobly replying,   *670*
"I won't, if that's your wish."
She glanced to Tarogo.
"I will not either," he
Affirmed quite huffily.
"Good." Her smile was relieved,   *675*
For at that moment she
Had what she hadn't had
For a long time – the hope
They wouldn't betray her
And renounce their promise.   *680*
Outside, the old woman
Walked on the compressed earth
To the clearing's boundary.
She bent to pick up twigs,
And other fuel supplies,   *685*
Somehow feeling content.
Within her head she heard
The words Yukei had said.
'Within my eyes alone
Are these troubles of mine.'   *690*
She plucked a broken stick.
'Be happy, and all that
You encounter will be

Just as filled with that joy.'
She paused, catching a glance   *695*
Of her own hand at work.
In the light of the moon,
The other hand came up
And spread wrinkled fingers
Over their counterparts.   *700*
Both hands glowed and now seemed
As alive as Yukei
Had been in the firelight.
Here she contemplated:
'I have the chance to live   *705*
Life in a better way.'
She caressed her arms and
Lifted them in the air.
To her came well-being,
And there, under the moon,   *710*
Did she begin to dance.
One foot gracefully stepped
In front of the other,
And through her feet, up came
The presence of the Earth.   *715*
Within, tranquility
Fused form with her movements.
Footsteps, heartbeats became
One with the larger part
Of the un-trying part   *720*
That comes from existence.
Serenity moved her;
Grace not imitated,
But in her metamorphed
To remembrance of All.   *725*
Just then, within the house,

Tarogo had woken
When the old woman's sounds
Of happy chattering
Had interrupted sleep.   730
Turned over now, he tried
To fall asleep once more,
But the bodily pain
Rumbling from his famished
Stomach kept him alert.   735
What's more, it kept his brain
As restless as his gut.
His rationale spun that,
'She said she'd make breakfast
Once the morning appeared' —   740
Like iron to magnet,
His glance flew over to
The one restricted place —
'So in there must be where
She's hiding all her food.'   745
Outside, her hands caressed
Her arms 'round and around
While she swayed to her song.
One foot dropping before
The other as he went,   750
Tarogo now tiptoed
Across the earthen floor.
The moon made her shadows
Fluid across the grass,
One foot 'fore the other,   755
And grace in one body
– In ground, and light, and life –
Crept into her being.
One foot 'fore the other

Took Tarogo to the   *760*
Only forbidden door.
One finger, and then two
Grasped the frame, and could slide
The door slowly open.
One moment needed more,   *765*
For eyes could see nothing
Inside the dark chamber,
But once he stepped aside
The light found its way in
To show to Tarogo   *770*
Shadows like piles of bones.
He tugged the door harder,
And there fell to his feet
A half-devoured head
Still shrieking with just one   *775*
Terrified eye socket.
Decomposing flesh stung
Deep in Tarogo's nose
As he looked upon horrors
In overpowering shock.   *780*
Stumbling backwards, his legs
Collapsed from under him,
So he was left to drag
Himself from the dire sight,
Fingernails clawing dirt.   *785*
Finally, he inhaled,
Sucking in just one draught
Before returning it
To the night as a scream.
The old woman halted,   *790*
Hands still raised in the air,
Her eyes clouding over

As she looked to the house.
Her breathless cry pleaded,
"No. For once, just one no."   795
And 'No!' escaped her heart
As a single tear fell
Through the moon's frigid light;
Fell 'fore hate crippled her.
She brought down her hands and   800
Watched them as they grew long,
Spiteful and ferocious,
The nails sprung like razors
To slice up lying men.
Her arms burst with muscles,   805
The skin dead like leather
But pulsating dark red
From the ogre's rage-filled
Heart forcing the crone's blood
To every blistering pore.   810
Her jaws split wide apart
As new teeth cut her gums
With fangs that dribbled down
Her own blood on her chin.

~ * ~ * ~ * ~ * ~ * ~ * ~ * ~

Yukei woke with a start.   815
Tarogo's face hovered
Above his with a fear
The likes he'd never seen.
"Ogre.... She's an ogre,"
The servant said lowly.   820
But to Yukei's confused
And sleep-choked reply of

"Who," Tarogo shouted:
"The woman's a demon –
She kills and eats people!"   *825*
In a daze from which it
Appeared hard to ascend,
Yukei climbed to his feet
And followed to the place
Tarogo was pointing.   *830*
At the bloody threshold
The master understood,
Recoiling in horror.
Quickly he realized
The poor trapped soul of   *835*
The human being must
Be the *Oni-baba*
Local children speak of
To frighten each other
On the long winter nights –   *840*
The Harridan Demon
From legend immortal.
Tarogo had scrambled
Back up upon his feet.
"Wait!" Yukei called out, but   *845*
The servant was too scared
To be hindered just by
Commands from his master;
And to the front door ran.
There he paused, hands in frame,   *850*
Breath panting outside air.
His eyes searched frantically
For the least little hint
Of where the woman was;
And so, seeing nothing,   *855*

He bolted through the door.
He ran to the clearing
And leaped into the field.
But as he leapt, his back   860
Began curiously
To feel moistened with pain.
His eyes turned just in time
To see the ogre's claws
Glistening in the moonlight,   865
Slashing his back once more.
And again, they ripped his
Flesh with no real mercy.
His head still turned to her,
Tarogo's one surprise   870
Was looking into the
Demon's contorted face:
Was pity in its eyes...?
Just as pain reached his mind,
Those monstrous hands struck out,   875
This time not letting go,
But anchoring deep in
The servant's ribs and spine.
In agony, he flinched
From the teeth biting him,   880
And felt his own blood pour
Like hot rage down the breast
Of the Oni-baba.
Yukei came to the door,
Knowing he lacked the time   885
To do anything for
A man he truly liked;
A man he then watched die
And leave the world as less

Than any person should.   *890*
In his own heart he fought
To regain self-control,
For he knew he needed
To conquer fear if he
Was to confront the *thing*   *895*
The old woman had let
Take possession of her.
It was the woman, who
Was still deep inside, he
Needed to assist him.   *900*
The demon spotted him –
Its eyes like blind revenge.
The unearthly creature
Leaped from the field's tall grass,
And on sightless feet, flew   *905*
Towards him in the house.
He jumped to the far wall,
Pressing hard against it
To flatten himself out.
The fiend had stopped its rush,   *910*
Waiting outside the door
As if to heighten fear.
Yukei shouted at it:
"Old woman, just listen –
Don't let the spirit break   *915*
Your agreement with it.
I kept my word to you;
Did not open that door.
You said 'No'; I obeyed."
He whispered on softly,   *920*
"Woman, fight for yourself."
The demon ran inside,

Fueled by hateful anger,
But the old woman fought,
And because her own heart   925
– Thanks to Yukei's teachings –
Had emptied of hatred,
The ogre was weakened.
It made it halfway 'cross
The hardpacked earthen floor   930
– With arms outstretched to slash –
When the old woman took
Back controlling her life.
Mere feet in front of him,
The beast fell to the ground,   935
Desperately mauling dirt
To try and get at him.
But then, most quietly,
The old woman's features
Began to reappear.   940
Her arms reached out to him,
As if beckoning him.
After he swallowed hard
To bravely steel himself,
He leaned down cautiously,   945
Soft-touching her shoulder.
She didn't move, so he
Gently rolled her over.
He saw her leg was bent
Backwards into a flap,   950
Snapped in many places.
She then opened her eyes,
And from between those slits,
Yukei witnessed placid
Gratitude escaping.   955

As she breathed her last breath,
He held onto her tight
So she'd not die alone
And with his simple act,
Shattered the demon's dream. *960*